I0499894

INTERVIEW
PREPARATION

How to Improve your Job Interview skills and Be Yourself.
Stop Worrying and Be More Positive with Amazing Interview
Answers

JIM HUNTING

Copyright © 2019 –
All rights reserved.

The content contained within this book may not be reproduced, duplicated or transmitted without direct written permission from the author or the publisher.

Under no circumstances will any blame or legal responsibility be held against the publisher, or author, for any damages, reparation, or monetary loss due to the information contained within this book. Either directly or indirectly.

Legal Notice:

This book is copyright protected. This book is only for personal use. You cannot amend, distribute, sell, use, quote or paraphrase any part, or the content within this book, without the consent of the author or publisher.

Disclaimer Notice:

Please note the information contained within this document is for educational and entertainment purposes only. All effort has been executed to present accurate, up to date, and reliable, complete information. No warranties of any kind are declared or implied. Readers acknowledge that the author is not engaging in the rendering of legal, financial, medical or professional advice. The content within this book has been derived from various sources. Please consult a licensed professional before attempting any techniques outlined in this book.

By reading this document, the reader agrees that under no circumstances is the author responsible for any losses, direct or indirect, which are incurred as a result of the use of information contained within this document, including, but not limited to, — errors, omissions, or inaccuracies.

Table of Contents

INTRODUCTION

Interviewers are not super humans that can do all things. They may seem to wield more power than you because they can decide if you are hired or not, but at the end of the day, they are still human just like you. They are not infallible and make mistakes. You shouldn't put them on a pedestal and think that they are better than you. They are similar to you in many ways. They are susceptible to the same psychological and cognitive biases that you are. In that way, they can catch on to things that are seemingly minute, but reveal something important inside of the interviewee.

There are things that you can do to make yourself a more likable person who is going to be perceived as outgoing, friendly, and an overall pleasant person to be around. In the game of the interview process, this manipulation tool can help you land a job. Let's look at all the ways that you can work with the interviewer's psychology to get the job of your dreams.

1. Schedule your interview for late morning on Tuesday

Likely, this is a time when the interviewer has gone past the craze of Monday that can be stressful and time-consuming. Once Tuesday rolls around, things are much calmer and more relaxed.

If you can arrange for the interview to be late morning on a Tuesday, things should be pretty smooth. Still, you must work around the interviewer's schedule to make sure you have a good time, but when you can arrange the interview around your own, then you can choose a time that you think will work to your advantage; this is at the time when the interviewer is at their best, because that will score you more points, and you will likely have a better outcome.

2. Don't interview on the same day as the strongest candidates

Research has shown that the interviewers base their scores on the other interviewees who have been there on the same day. If you have a series of stronger candidates before your interview, then you will likely be scored down and not get the job. However, if you are after a series of weaker candidates, then likely your score will go up. You may not know who is interviewing and when, but if you have any knowledge beforehand of the people interviewing, then you should choose to come in on a day that has less qualified applicants than you, because you can score more points and have a better result, which could put you in the running for the second or third round of interviews that may come after.

3. Choose what you wear very carefully

Research has shown that orange is the absolute worst color you could possibly wear to an interview, so you should definitely avoid wearing that color. A CareerBuilder survey revealed that many applicants preferred wearing blue, because it indicates that you are a team player and can work well with others. Whereas black suggests that you have leadership potential. Gray suggests that you are logical and analytical. White indicates that you are organized. Brown means you are dependable. Red shows that you can exercise power in your job.

4. Work your hand motions as they will reveal a lot about your character

You should hold your palm outward to show a sign of sincerity, because that will demonstrate that you are a man or woman of integrity and can share well. You can also hold your hand to make the shape of a church steeple, which indicates that you are confident. Conversely, you should not hold your palm downward, because it can indicate a sign of dominance. Don't hide your hands, because it may seem like you're trying to hide something. Also, if you tap your fingers, you are displaying a sign of impatience, and if you fold your arms, you may be indicating disappointment. If you do these actions, then you can start focusing on projecting the most positive image possible.

5. Find something that you have in common with the interviewer

Often, the similarity attraction hypothesis comes into play when you can find something that you have in common with the interviewer. Maybe you're wearing a similar style as the interviewer; you can emphasize that. Or, if your interviewer mentions something about a recent basketball game and you can chime in about it, then you can continue the conversation. You can also bring it back to the interviewer's interests as you go about the process. That can resonate well with a person, because it can seem a little bit like emotional flattery, and you can help the interviewer feel like you appreciate them and could work well with them.

6. Body language mirroring

One way to flatter your interviewer is to do exactly what they are doing during the interview. If they are sitting back in their chair, then you should do the same, or if they are sitting up straight and leaning forward toward you, do as they do. It can help show that you can conform to their pattern of behavior and that you can adapt to different environments.

7. Give compliments to the company without self-promotion

Another thing you should be careful about is offering compliments to your interviewer or the organization. You don't want to sound like you're flattering in order to help your personal profile. That could backfire easily and make it more likely for you to not get the job. Be wary about how you give compliments to the organization that you're looking into working for.

8. Be excited about it

It has been shown that the more enthusiastic and excited you are about the role and the interview, the higher the chances you will get asked back to another interview or even get the position. There are many applicants who are looking to get the job, but you should try to find ways that you can project your excitement and energy, because that can definitely work in your favor. When you show that you are highly engaged in the interview, you demonstrate an interest in the company, which could help you in the whole process.

Examples

Qualities to describe Nick: Intelligent, warm, friendly, talented, and hardworking, but slightly overly confident.

Qualities that describe Frank: Overly confident, hardworking, intelligent, warm, and friendly.

The two candidates are very similar in the adjectives that are used for them, but one is clearly better than the other due to the order of the adjectives that are ascribed to them. It makes a difference in the interview process, because we always seek out the positive first in a candidate and can easily sidestep the potential drawbacks within a person.

13. Emphasize your efforts over your success

One thing that you can do in the interview is to emphasize your hard work and dedication over the success that you have experienced. Instead of saying, "I am successful," you can say, "I struggled during this time with XYZ, but I was able to accomplish XYZ after a lot of hard work and effort." When you do so, you demonstrate kindness, amicability, relatability, and humility, all of which are positive attributes of a potential colleague. Such attributes will help the interviewer to sift through the various candidates and find a humble but likable character who could be a good fit for their organization.

14. Prepare to ad-lib and go off script

One thing that many interviewers expect is for their interviewees to have a pre-programmed script in their minds, which will lead the interview in a certain direction, ultimately to land the person the job. However, this is not always the way it needs to be. There should be a certain amount of natural spontaneity in the conversation that makes it less canned and predictable. Instead, you should say things like, "Let me tell you what's not on my resume…" When you can bring new information that is not evident on the resume, then you can demonstrate what knowledge and expertise you bring to the table. You can do so by wowing your interviewer with the variety of information that you can present to them without being so predictable that they know every word that you are about to say; that is just not very interesting.

15. Ask the interviewer why they invited you to the interview

Another key tip for the process is preparing to ask the interviewer why they brought you in. It shows initiative and humility, but you automatically draw attention to why the interviewers want to talk to you about a potential position with them. This can play to your strength, because then the interviewer will see you in a positive light.

To conclude, show what you can do to prepare for an interview and what you can do to prepare psychologically, as well as to think about the way an interviewer will perceive you when you arrive at the interview. Furthermore, you should play up your strengths so that you will be viewed in a favorable way. That will help you greatly in the application process and make you a candidate who stands out.

CHAPTER 1

JOB HUNTING

Job search is the most difficult game there is. There are many reasons why this is so. Here are a few of them:

1. It is a game that requires us to play in a certain way.

2. Most jobseekers know that they are supposed to sell, or promote themselves, but they hate the idea of selling. How can anyone perform well at a task they despise?

3. All job seekers are selling, whether they want to or not, but virtually everyone of them has adopted the worst possible sales style, as I will soon illustrate.

4. Jobseekers are required to sell the most complex, hardest-to-sell product in the world—themselves. This is difficult because most people are uncomfortable promoting themselves.

5. Successful job search requires us to understand the value we represent, and then confidently express this value. But it is hard to be objective about ourselves. Most jobseekers struggle to understand what their strengths are for many

weeks.

6. Jobseekers are required to sell this incredibly complex product under the most pressure-packed circumstance: the job interview. This isn't a seven-game series where you can lose three games and still advance. If you lose in the first round, bye-bye. You may have been a close second, but there is no medal for second place.

7. The job interview is a complex sale and few people—even salespeople—understand this approach. Most jobseekers have never received an hour of training in the art of complex sales. Worse yet, there are few resources that do a good job covering this subject.

8. Finally, the game requires you to be upbeat and confident, even though you may have just received the leveling, painful blow of job loss.

Is there any wonder why most un-coached jobseekers, when they are handed the ball, take off in the wrong direction? Sending an untrained person to an interview is like taking someone who has never driven a car and giving them the keys, pointing out the location of the brakes, accelerator and steering wheel, and setting them free on the German autobahn for their maiden voyage. Godspeed!

GOOD NEWS FOR THOSE WHO HATE SELLING

The complex sales approach that you will learn from this book has the following great advantage: It does not feel like selling to either you, or to the hiring authority. This is by design, because people love buying, but don't like being sold.

I remember taking a potential customer, and her team, to dinner, escorting them through a plant tour the next day, followed by our "sales presentation." We presented problems we had uncovered and their potential solutions. We spoke about their goals and how our product might lead to their achievement.

Lunch and a short walk to a waiting limo ended our time together. Before the buying authority entered the limo that was headed to O'Hare airport, she turned to me and said words I've never forgotten, "I've been with you for two days, and you've yet to try and sell me anything."

I smiled and said, "It's all my fault. Have a nice flight back home." But while I said that I thought, "I've been selling you from the moment you arrived." It did not feel that way, but she was sold. She did buy our system.

If you master this system you won't feel like you have been selling anyone, and that is just one of the many reasons why the system works. Remember, Jack was and is an engineer. Engineers tend not to like selling or have a strong urge to pursue a career in sales. Yet Jack adopted my approach and, as we will find out later, is still using some of its techniques to be successful in his new job.

MASTERING THE GAME

I hate golf and I can't understand why people take golfing vacations. I went to St. Andrews' University for my junior year abroad. It's the birthplace of golf. Golfers who learn of this always ask me, "Did you play on the Old Course?" Their eyes sparkle with delight, but their glimmer dies quickly when I answer, "Nope. Never even made it to the driving range or the putting green. But I did drink my fair share of pints at the Niblick." The Niblick is a pub that is very close to the Old Course.

What stands behind my aversion? I stink at golf. I don't like it and it doesn't like me. That is one of the reasons why people hate interviewing: They stink at it, and know this deep inside, even if they cannot consciously admit it to themselves.

If you seriously apply yourself to master the lessons in this book, then you will master the game of job search, and this can make interviewing enjoyable. I know this firsthand. I got to the point where I enjoyed interviewing. But I wanted to see if this was true for Jack, after two grueling days of eighteen interviews. His experience would be something of an acid test. So, I asked him if he enjoyed the experience and he replied:

As far as the interviewing experience, surprisingly I did have a positive experience. I felt very prepared and felt confident that I could convey my experience and skills sets in a very effective manner (clear, concise and with stories).

Note how he continues to emphasize stylistic points like clarity, eliminating wordiness, and using stories. He learned valuable lessons about how to communicate effectively, and his continual repetition of these insights indicated he was not going to forget them.

Jack's experience reveals a key to job search success. We need to make the interviewing process enjoyable by mastering it, and by getting rid of our conventional, simple sales pitch.

THE SIMPLE SALE

Here is the crowning irony of job search: Those jobseekers who hate the idea of selling are unwittingly adopting the worst possible sales style. They typically use a simple sales approach that I will briefly describe so that it can be avoided at all costs.

In the simple sale there is typically one decision maker, because the price tag for the simple-sale's item, or service, is low. When the price is low, the risks of making a bad-buying decision are also low. If the decision maker purchases something that doesn't work out, his attitude is, "No big deal." He learns from his inexpensive mistake and moves on. For this reason there is no need to waste the time of multiple decision makers, or put a complex decision-making process in place. There is no committee making a buying decision in simple sales.

The simple sales approach looks like this:

Salesperson: Hi, I'm Bill. I represent Acme, Inc., the ballpoint pen suppliers for most of the school systems in the state. The reason why we're twice as large as our next largest competitor is because of the quality of the product and the low cost. Most of my customers are placing their annual stocking orders right now, have you placed yours?

Buyer: Nope.

Salesperson: So how many pens do you need to fill your stocking order? [Followed by...] That order would cost ____. If you place your order now you can get free shipping and it will arrive by next week. Deal?

Buyer: Maybe. I'll think about it.

Salesperson: That's fine. But if you think about it, you've got a hundred more important things to think about. How about we take this item off your to-do list and get you set up for the school year with the best quality pens at a discounted price?

Buyer: You're probably right. Use this P.O. number.

I rattle off a few of the most impressive facts and then I close, close, close. Ask for the order! If an objection arises, I answer it and then close, close, close. However, in the complex sales process I never asked for the order. Not once, much less three times.

Now let's apply this simple sales approach to the job interview to see what it looks like.

THE SIMPLE JOB INTERVIEW

The simple sales style can work during an interview, but only for a simple job opportunity. These are the low-skilled, low-paying jobs where one person meets the candidate and often makes the hiring decision on the spot. The downside of making a bad decision is low so no hiring committee is ever formed.

Take, for example, a dishwashing job. The interview might go like this:

Kitchen Manager: You here for the dishwashing job?

Interviewee: Yep.

Kitchen Manager: We pay the minimum wage and the hours are Tuesday through Saturday night, from five in the evening to one in the morning.

Interviewee: Cool. I work hard and show up on time. Do I start tonight?

Offer a few reasons why you should be hired and ask for the job. This is a very direct and rational approach, and for the simple job opportunity this makes sense. The hiring authority is exposed to little risk if he makes a bad decision. If things don't pan out, then another warm body can quickly be found. Emotion will only enter the equation when the stakes are higher, the compensation and responsibilities are greater, and it becomes a higher-risk, higher-reward decision. Then the process becomes more complex. Several people interview multiple candidates, and the "sale" is no longer simple.

JOBSEEKERS SELLING POORLY

They interview as if driven by this philosophy: *Whoever*

presents the most reasons, and the best reasons, will win the interviewing contest.

Whether they've thought about it or not, they act like the hiring decision is a rational one. After all, how could something so important to their life and career be irrational? "Doesn't the hiring authority want to hire the best?" their thought process goes. "And don't I need to show them I am the best by piling up the evidence that this is so?"

If the interviewer was a computer that could hear every reason why we are the best candidate, immediately calculate its worth, and simultaneously compare these weighted reasons to those of the other four candidates, then they would choose us if our qualifications outweighed our competition's. But the hiring authority is human—most of the time—and he can't keep up with weighing the information, organizing it, remembering it, etc., before more arrives.

Now multiply the impact of this data-dumping style times five (you and your four competitors). By the end of the fifth interview, the hiring authority's ears are bleeding and his head is about to explode. He forgets what has been said and who said it. The continuous stream of facts and data creates a data fog, and all of the candidates disappear in it. The exhausted interviewer struggles to associate resumes with the people he met mere hours ago.

THE CAUSES OF THE HIRING-DECISION-EFFECT

This rational, simple-sales approach doesn't work, because the complex hiring decision is caused by emotions, not reasons. If we are to cause a hiring decision, then we need to employ these emotional causes.

Let's compare the hiring of dishwashers to the hiring of professionals. With dishwashers there was a low risk-reward element in the decision. But when it comes to hiring professionals, a higher risk-reward relationship is in play.

If, for example, I hire a disruptive person for my marketing team, someone who destroys my team's chemistry and is disrespectful to authority figures, then I have not only made my life miserable, but I've hurt the productivity of the team, my company and my standing within it. I will now appear to be a poor judge of character and an ineffective team builder. Conversely, when I hire someone who exceeds all expectations, it makes my life easier as a manager, and it reflects well on me.

The risk and reward of hiring professionals introduces emotion into the decision-making process. I fear making a mistake. I don't hire someone who I cannot trust, or who makes me feel uncomfortable. I hire people I like and who I want to be around.

PERCEPTION AND EMOTION

One of the reasons why emotions cause hiring decisions is because they shape perception. Favorable emotions can create a filter that keeps the hiring authority from seeing our weaknesses, while negative feelings can keep them from seeing our strengths. For example, when our interviewing style gets an interviewer to like us, this influences their perception in ways that favor us, because "perception is affected not only by what people *expect* to see; it is also colored by what they *want* to see."

The hiring authority looks for reasons to hire the candidate they like the most. They begin to see "what they *want* to see." When candidates are liked, then everything they say or do is colored in a positive way. There is a psychological reason why love is blind: We see what we want to see.

Let's return to the woman who said I had yet to sell her anything. She did not realize that the reason why we took her and her team up to the top of the Hancock Building for drinks, then out to a nice dinner, was to generate positive feelings toward us. Then, when we made our presentation, we did not present facts and data, but solutions to problems that caused painful feelings. In short, I was using emotions to cause the buying-decision-effect.

Once we understand the importance of emotion we will take a less rational approach to our quest for employment. We will stop focusing on the limited rational mind, and will make our appeal to another mental system that is more emotional. The way it impacts decision-making, communication, and perception will change our job-search course.

CHAPTER 2

SECURING AN INTERVIEW

Proper planning and perseverance will be the key to securing a quality number of interviews. It is vitally important to maintain a positive attitude throughout the process of securing interviews. There will undoubtedly be times during this phase of your job search that you will become very frustrated and want to quit. However, giving up at this point in the process will get you nowhere except back to where you started.

It's a common practice for many companies including search firms not to respond to your letters, resumes and phone calls during this part of your job search. Unless they have an interest in your background, they are simply inundated with resumes and lack the resources to respond to every applicant. Learn to expect rejection at this point of your search and try not to take it too personally. Continue on with your search and do not give up just because several people have not responded or simply indicated that there is no interest in your background.

Rejection: Simply Just a Way of Saying No, For Now

Rejection is simply a "No" answer, for now. By properly

following up on a rejection letter, you may find that the company does have a need for your skills and invite you in for an interview. Should you receive a rejection letter pertaining to a position for which you have applied, you should immediately write a letter back to the employer addressing it to the hiring authority. Indicate in your letter that you understand and respect their decision, however you feel confident that you may be an asset to their company. Be specific and explain how your experience and background can benefit their company. Indicate that you have done a great deal of research and have respect for their company's products or services as well as their corporate goals. Follow-up your letter with a telephone call to the hiring authority. It is very important that your letter and phone call be sent to a key decision-maker for the position you seek.

Speculation and the Law of Averages

Your ability to find and secure the job of your choice is a speculative process. You can increase your chances of a successful search by adopting and working with a principle called "The Law of Averages." A career search method that utilizes the "Law of Averages" is what I have termed "The Bullet Approach." This approach is based upon a systematic method of sending resumes to key decision makers using your target list of fifteen to twenty companies. By using this approach, you dramatically increase your chances of securing interviews with companies specific to your interest and skill match. If your particular skills and experience match those of a company you have targeted, the opportunity for a successful match increases significantly.

Another career search method that is often used but provides poor results is called "The Shotgun Approach." This approach also uses "The Law of Averages," but does not use the law properly to achieve a statistical advantage. "The Shotgun Approach" works on a principle similar to that of a real shotgun where a large number of pellets are propelled out of the gun in somewhat of a uniform pattern hoping to hit part of the target. Applied as a job search method, you literally present as many resumes as possible to companies hoping for a response. It is nearly impossible to effectively follow-up with such a large number of companies versus the fifteen to twenty I have advocated with "The Bullet Approach."

When you apply "The Bullet Approach" to your job search, you are not limited to the initial fifteen to twenty companies you have selected. It is wise however to try and limit the number you target at any one time. If you target too many companies you may not be able to properly research and follow-up with each company. As you begin to follow-up with companies on your initial target list, continue the process of researching other potential companies of interest. Begin to add other companies to your target list in the same proportion of those you eliminate.

If you target a company where your experience and skills do not match a particular job profile, your chances of securing the position is limited. A job match is similar to an organ transplant, where there must be a near perfect tissue and blood type match. If there is no match, the body will reject the organ. For example, if you are a computer sales representative selling computer hard drives, the probability of securing a position with another computer company selling hardware is significantly enhanced. This opposed to trying to obtain a position outside your known field of selling chemicals to the food industry.

However, if you want to change careers, you will need to present and sell your talents and skills in a different manner. Suppose you have made the decision to seek a sales position with a company whose products are unfamiliar to you. Emphasize your sales skills, including your ability to build a business. Emphasize your sales achievements and all other related sales skills including your exceptional negotiating and closing abilities.

You have taken an important step in your job search by identifying and researching companies that meet your career requirements. The next step in your job search will be to secure an interview with the proper hiring authority at each of your target companies. Making contact with a hiring authority is an important key to the success of your search. View this essential step of the process as if you were a private investigator trying to locate a missing person. Who are you trying to locate? What is that person's name, title and function within their business?

If you are a sales representative seeking a sales position you should make contact with the Vice President or Director of Sales. If however these are positions you seek, direct your contact to an Executive Vice President or President of the company. The most effective method for making contact with company managers is to start high on the company's organizational chart, i.e., President, Vice President, Director, etc. It is always beneficial to be able to indicate to a Director or Regional Manager that the Vice President or President of their company has asked you to make contact with them.

This type of referral represents a higher level of authority and gives you instant credibility with mid level management. This important telephone call enables you to establish a one on one conversation with the proper hiring authority. The more personal contact you have with the hiring authority either by telephone, mail, email, personal meetings, etc., is key to securing the position you desire.

Develop a system to follow-up on each telephone call to a potential employer or contact. It may be beneficial to create a spreadsheet on your computer using a program such as Microsoft's Excel. Create your own form indicating headings such as: Date, Contact, Title, Company, Address, Email, Web, Telephone and Fax numbers including a Purpose/Results section. In addition to developing a spreadsheet to track your contacts, there are a number of very sophisticated contact databases such as ACT, which are excellent tools for tracking your contacts and any action taken with them.

Because you have targeted fifteen to twenty companies you should make at least fifteen to twenty follow-up telephone calls after sending your resume. How well you handle each follow-up phone call to a proposed hiring authority may determine whether or not you will secure an interview.

Human Resources, Proceed with Extreme Caution!

You may want to make contact with the personnel office specifically with the Vice President, Director or Manager of Human Resources within the company you are interested. Proceed with extreme caution when making contact with a company's personnel department! A friend of mine commented during his job search that he often felt the personnel department was like a giant black hole, where everything was sucked in and nothing came out. Without entirely degrading personnel, as they do have a function, it is my view that you should initially avoid the personnel area. Your first contact should be the hiring authority and if they are interested in your background, personnel will be copied on your background and will become involved. It is my experience that individuals involved in the personnel department tend not to fully understand the intricacy of hiring, as this is only a small percentage of their total duties.

I have only had the pleasure of working with a few true professional personnel individuals who understand the complexity of hiring people. The problem is that most personnel managers do not view people as individuals, but rather as a stereotyped group of people called applicants or candidates. If you decide to send your resume to a company's personnel department, it is important to address your letter to a specific individual ideally a senior manager within the department rather than simply "Personnel."

As previously indicated, it is important to develop a system of follow-up with your company contacts. I often hear about job seekers sending out cover letters and resumes but never personally following up with a telephone call to their contact.

Your follow-up telephone call is one of the most important aspects of the job search. It enables you to establish a one on one conversation with the proposed hiring authority. Without direct personal contact with the hiring authority you will not be able to secure a position.

Before you make your initial follow-up call, I have found it very helpful to write out your proposed conversation. Your notes will act as a script that will assist you to stay focused on the purpose of your conversation. A key factor for any follow-up telephone call is to determine the purpose for your call. Realize that you are selling yourself, your skills and knowledge to the prospective employer. Ask yourself the question, what is my purpose for calling this person, and what do I hope to accomplish. Try to anticipate any questions the employer may ask you and what your response will be. If you have ever played chess, checkers or any other game requiring strategy, you understand that the ability to anticipate a challenger's move is an extremely important aspect of winning the game.

An example of an initial follow-up call after you have sent a cover letter and a resume to the hiring authority known as Mr. Robert Morris, Vice President of JEM Computer, Inc. may be as follows:

"Hello, Mr. Morris, my name is John Powell. I recently wrote to you regarding my background in the area of computer hardware sales, specifically in the area of high- resolution computer screens." (Your specific product or service experience stated should be of interest to Mr. Morris and his company.) "The purpose of my call is to introduce myself as a potential candidate for a sales position within your company. I recently sent you my resume. Do you have a moment where I might discuss with you how I can be an asset to your company?" Stop! Let Mr. Morris respond to your initial statements. A myriad of responses from Mr. Morris may follow your introductory statements. He may simply say, "Yes, I am in receipt of your resume, and although you have an excellent background, we do not have a position available at this time commensurate with your experience."

Don't give up at this point in your discussion. Ask Mr. Morris if he foresees, in the near future, a position where your background in the area of high-resolution computer screens may become available. Consider the fact that it is possible that the position you seek with JEM Computer, Inc. may open up in the near future. If Mr. Morris says, "Yes, in fact a position may be available in about a month, however this particular job is within another division." Ask him what the specific duties of that position are. Who does the position report to? Can you speak directly with that person? Is it okay to indicate that Mr. Morris referred you to that individual?

In addition, ask Mr. Morris if he is aware of another company that may be expanding or have specific personnel needs where your background would be a potential fit. If Mr. Morris recommends a company to you, ask him if he has any contacts within the company. If he refers you to a particular contact, ask him if it is okay to indicate that he was the source of the referral. This approach will give you instant credibility with the referred company and may be the key to securing a new position.

Finally, it is always wise to send a thank you note to Mr. Morris expressing your appreciation for the time he spent with you regarding his company and your potential role within his company. You should also express your continued interest in his company and a desire to speak with him further should a position become available. If Mr. Morris was able to refer you to another company, thank him for his referral as well.

Depending upon the level of rapport you have developed with Mr. Morris during your conversation, you may also want to ask him if he has some time to meet with you. You should indicate to him that you have done some research on his company and that it is a firm you are very interested in working for. Even though there isn't an open position at the present time, you would like to learn more about his company should a position become available in the near future. If you are able to arrange a meeting with Mr. Morris, treat it as any other interview you have secured. You may be surprised by the results. Mr. Morris may like you, and he might create a position for you within his company. If he does not have a position commensurate with your background at this time, you may want to ask him if it would be okay for you to speak with his Director of Computer Sales, Sales Manager, or both individuals. They may be able to direct you to other contacts within the industry that may lead you to other job search leads.

The larger and more enhanced your network becomes, the probability of securing a position with a company or organization that you desire becomes greater. It is important to remember that locating and securing a job is a calculated numbers game where the law of averages is always a factor for success. If you make contact with the proper hiring authorities within a select number of targeted companies, your chances of landing a position is high. Put into practice the motto of my Executive Search firm of "Quality versus Quantity," and you will succeed in your job search.

CHAPTER 3

RESEARCHING
THE ORGANIZATION

Before your interview, find out as much as you can about the company. It will help you answer their questions better and think of good questions for the interviewer at the end. There's a wealth of information available online that you can use. Follow our top tips to gather information.

- *Visit the company website.* The company's website is the first place to look when doing your research. Most companies have an "About Us" page where you can read their mission statement, history and what they say about their company culture.

- *Use LinkedIn.* LinkedIn company profiles can give you plenty of information. You'll be able to see if you have any connections there who may be able to help you. You can also see new hires, promotions, company statistics and other jobs they have posted. Find your interviewer's profile to gain insight into their job and background.

- *Google the company.* Do a Google search for the company,

focusing on the web and news results. Have they recently achieved something noteworthy? What are the latest company developments? Avoid any bad press, or anything which gives a negative impression of the company.

- *Speak to your connections.* Do you know anyone who works there? Ask if they can help. Find out what they may know about the company that isn't in the news or available online. This will give you advantage over other candidates who don't have your connections.

- *Read the small print.* When you are on the company's website, use the sitemap to find pages that may not be easy to find. You'll be surprised how much information could be hidden away!

- *Speak to your recruitment agency.* If you secured this interview through an agency, speak to your consultant about the company. They will know a lot about them, as they would have worked and looked for candidates for them before.

1. Make a list. Think of things you may want to find out before you start. Here are a few examples:

2. How old is the company

3. How many people work for them?

4. How many countries do they operate in?

5. What are their main products and services?

6. Who are their customers?

7. Who are their competitors?

8. Where is their head office based?

9. What training programs do they offer?

10. What does their Annual Report or accounts say about the business?

- *Make some calls.* Call the company's human resources department and ask about the company. They may be willing to share some information with you.

- *Use social network sites.* See if they have a Twitter account or Facebook page. By liking them on Facebook or following them on Twitter, you will receive all of their updates and posts. See if they have a blog and read some of their posts.

What Are They Looking For?

There are three main things the interviewer wants to know, and your answers to these will depend on how you respond to other questions and how you act and react during the interview.

1. Can you do the job?

2. This relates to your skills, knowledge and experience, and when you have done similar roles before.

3. How will you do it?

4. This relates to your personal qualities, for example, whether you are good at speaking to customers, your networking abilities, if you keep calm under pressure, or what type of a manager you are.

5. Will you make the tea?

6. What we mean by this is "How will you fit in with the company culture and the rest of the team?" You will spend more time at work than you do with your family during the day, so a prospective line manager will be asking themselves, "Will this person get along with the team and me?" You and your colleagues don't have to be best friends but you do need to get on.

So how do you find out what exactly the company is looking for in an employee? The job description should give you an idea.

You can use this to structure your answers to show your interviewer that you are the right person for the role.

Let's say the job description is for an admin assistant who will work as part of a large team in the complaints department.

You can use your previous admin work experience to answer the first question. How you deal with customers, e.g., staying calm even when confronted am angry client, will answer the second question. Your ability to work with your teammates will answer the third question.

Technical Interview

If you're going for a role that requires a high level of technical knowledge, you might find yourself having to undergo a technical interview. It may also be in the form of a written test or presentation.

In each case, preparation is the key. You are unlikely to get the job if you cannot demonstrate your technical knowledge to the required level, under pressure.

Do not panic. Approach each problem logically. If you require further clarification, do not hesitate to ask, as this type of test may include impossible or "**trick**" questions. These are designed to assess your problem-solving skills and logical thought processes, as well as your technical knowledge.

Assessment Centre

This type of interview normally takes place over one or more days in a specially selected location. As a candidate, you could be subjected to different types of interviews.

You are also likely to take part in several group or individual activities. These can include mini-assault courses or group tasks, such as constructing items from provided materials within in a certain time frame. These activities will be used to assess your problem-solving skills, ability to perform under pressure and your communication, negotiation and teamwork skills.

You may be asked to give presentations to the group or to the panel of interviewers. You may also have to undergo written tests designed to assess your literacy, numeracy and technical knowledge. The company may also use psychometric testing to evaluate your personality.

This type of interview is extremely tough and is normally reserved for graduate and higher level positions. Rehearse for all types of interviews, do some IQ and psychometric tests, and brush up on your literacy, numeracy and problem-solving skills.

Tests and resources are readily available on the internet.

Keep in mind throughout the process that your performance is constantly being evaluated. Many companies will put on a lunch or dinner for candidates and interviewers in order to assess their social skills. If you are a smoker, do try and limit the number of breaks that you have and ensure you freshen up after having one.

Second interview

If you do well enough to go through the first interview, you might then be asked to return for a second one. By now the company will have a shortlist of potential candidates and may need to whittle this down to make an offer to one candidate. The second interview could take the form of any of the interview types already discussed, so be ready for anything.

If you have faced assessment centers or panel interviews in the first round, the second interview will more likely be to see how you will integrate into the team. You may even have the opportunity to visit the place where you will be working or to meet some of your potential team members.

Treat each succeeding interview with as much attention as the first. Do not assume that the next interviewer knows what you told the first one. Be prepared to repeat yourself, if necessary. Do not get complacent and think that as this is your second or third interview, you are a definite shoo-in for the job. Yes, you are one step closer, but you still need to give it 100%.

CHAPTER 4

INTERVIEW SKILLS THAT WILL GET YOU HIRED

In competing with so many applicants for any given job and throughout the hiring process, what does a hiring manager look for which will differentiate you from other job candidates?

1. Knowledge of the Company

In the same way a hiring manager is interviewing you and investing in getting to know you, and whether or not you're a good fit for their company, a hiring manager is also looking to see if you've also done your homework. Take the time to research the companies you are applying to work for, including their strengths and weaknesses; and demonstrate this by asking intelligent questions about the company.

3. Great Attitude

Most people do not like to work with or hire a grouch. Put on a smile, develop an authentic "can do" attitude, and let this shine through when you interact with hiring managers. Remember, if the hiring manager doesn't enjoy being around you and your attitude, they can be fairly sure your would-be co-workers also wouldn't enjoy you, and you probably won't make the cut.

4. Team Player

Employers are interested in hiring those who work well with others and who recognize that greatness is never achieved in a silo. Demonstrating that you are a team player to a prospective employer is powerful. As you share your past work experiences, demonstrate your ability to work in a team by highlighting the strengths of the teams you've worked on in the past and praise others for their contributions in addition to mentioning your own.

5. Flexibility

Employers want to hire professionals who can flex. A person who is stuck in their ways and doesn't demonstrate adaptability tends to be harder to work with. This is especially important in today's corporate climate where job scopes change and evolve day by day to meet a company's needs. Employers know they can get more mileage out of a professional who can adapt to a variety of job requirements and company needs.

6. Growth Mindset

This is perhaps the most misunderstood and yet the most

important skill that will affect the impression you leave with a hiring manager. A growth mindset is not meant to indicate you are a professional intent on growth within an organization, upward mobility, and a desire to advance in your position. Rather, a growth mindset means you look at your job, your company and your work responsibilities with the eye of someone intent on personal growth and development. You are a professional who will continue learning, perfecting your skills and learning new ones, and someone who is agile and capable of growth and change. You may have held the same position for ten years, but every single year you enhance your ability to do your job better, more efficiently, and to a higher degree of professionalism. A growth mindset is less about career advancement and more about demonstrating that you are a flexible, adaptable, forward thinking professional.

7. Self-Starter (Highly Motivated)

Self-motivation may be one of a hiring manager's most sought after attributes in a candidate because it directly correlates to how a hiring manager will need to invest their own time and effort in managing an employee. Employees who are motivated on their own and don't require constant supervision and prompting from their manager are more likely to be low-maintenance and highly productive additions to a team.

8. Excellent Soft Skills

Beyond how your background, education, experience, and industry knowledge qualifies you for a position, hiring managers want to know if you have the right soft skills to be a good fit for their team. These are the skills that most degrees and years in an industry won't teach you, but they are what can make or break your ability to convince a hiring manager you are a worthwhile addition. Respectful, hardworking, dependable, positive, organized, confident, works well under pressure, effective communicator, and a problem solver are a few examples of highly desirable soft skills.

9. Ability to add Value to the Organization

Think about a time you've purchased a vehicle. Beyond the year, make and model, you are interested in the additional assets a car possesses which will add value to your purchase – a sunroof, a backup camera, remote keyless entry, for example. Presenting yourself to a hiring manager is like showing yourself off as a car to a potential buyer. If you can demonstrate value in yourself as a candidate, including attributes like superior knowledge, skills or job-related abilities, you have a better chance of showing a hiring manager that you can add value to a company. What is the skill or attribute you have that will make you invaluable to a hiring manager? Find that answer and then sell that in your interview and on your resume as a way of differentiating yourself from the pack of other candidates.

CHAPTER 5

THE SECRET OF INTERVIEW ETIQUETTE

Principles of Interview Etiquette

I cannot think of a situation more difficult than walking into an interview room with a stranger who has the upper hand and who questions everything you say or do. It is easy to lose your composure and confidence, which then makes everything else go haywire. As you prepare to attend the next interview, remember to equip yourself with business etiquette as it is a core pillar to successful interviews.

Your etiquette determines whether or not you get to the next level of the recruitment process. Most job candidates spend much of their time and energy thinking about their skills and qualifications to present to the interviewer and forget about personal conduct. Good manners determine the success of a business relationship since they determine how you establish rapport with other people. Your manner of behavior toward others is equally important as your résumé and any kind of experience. It is no surprise, therefore, that recruiters are interested in individuals who will fit within their business family.

The following guidelines reflect the principles of interview etiquette that show you how to avoid some mistakes job hunters have made and which derail them from reaching their goal.

How to greet your interviewers

Interviewers are most often referred to by their first name. Chances of offending someone by referring to them by their first name are minimal since it is the universal standard of meeting someone for the first time. However, calling someone by their last name shows a sense of respect and it directly tells them that you consider them important. Remember that the employer is looking for suggestions that you will be easy to work with, fully understanding the organizational management structure and respecting it.

Table talk

After greeting, the interviewer should remain standing until or unless you are asked to sit. Once you are offered a seat, refrain from feeling comfortable to the point of placing your belongings, such as a handbag, on the table. Be humble enough to place them under your chair or beside your legs. Only a professional binder should be placed on the table near you.

Remember to turn down the offer of a drink politely if one is offered. Finally, sit up properly without moving your feet around.

Ensure your cell phone is completely off

An interview is definitely one of the most crucial gatherings in your life and a phone distraction is not worth ruining such a meeting. Interviewers are keen to notice a phone's vibration; thus, it should be totally off. If possible, do not enter the interview room with your phone. At this moment there is nothing more important than your conversation with your potential employer. They will want to know if you can serve their clients without being distracted by your own personal gadget. Therefore, make sure to avoid the distraction at all costs.

Let the company take the lead during the conversation

Sometimes your interviewer may be laid back or soft-spoken, which may tempt you to get things going. You may start assuming the lead position and you eventually become inconsequential. Refrain from giving in to the temptation and let the interviewer take the lead regardless of their style. Go silent and do not look bored whenever they go silent. After all, you have nothing to worry about if you are well prepared. So just relax. Talking too much is a common mistake that interviewees make. It is easy to begin explaining things that are uncalled for when your employer is a person of few words.

Do not talk over the speaker

The most disturbing aspect in an interview is stepping into the interviewer's last two to three words of a statement and talking over without even extending the courtesy to letting them finish their statement. In this chapter, it comes off as a principle of etiquette. Show that you would respect the management and that you have good listening skills, which are so valuable in today's business world.

Take notes during the interview

One of the items that you should bring with you into an interview room is a professional-looking binder. Remember to make it useful during the conversation. Taking notes indicates that you are candidly interested in the job and the company, and it also helps you to pose a query when you are given a chance. Talking of an official folder, invest in one that looks first class. Do not use an electronic gadget such as a tablet to take notes in the interview. Such gadgets can only be used if you are interviewing for an Information Technology position or something similar. Also, remember that providing your professional references and résumé copies is a positive note.

Chase the position tirelessly even if you feel like the interview has already gone wrong

It is not unusual for someone to be having a rough time during an interview and to even create conclusions about the company, which may impact their ability to deliver the best version of themselves. The best thing you can do during such a time is to maintain professionalism and finish the interview without showing any signs of backing down. Remember you are not being forced to take this job, after all. You are still in the driver's seat in the end since you can always turn down an offer or respectfully withdraw from the process. Job candidates can be fond of prejudice toward the interviewers and they end up regretting it later. Ensure that you have collected all possible facts before making an ultimate judgment about the organization. Leave the interviewers with a good impression of you as it could pay back later in unimaginable ways. Imagine having poorly interviewed with this employer's biggest client who is now your boss.

Remember that your interview is not over until you walk out of the gate

From the moment you walk through the gate, how you talk to the receptionist or any other person, including the premises' cleaners, matters a lot in your hiring process. Some employers have taken time to ask parties such as the receptionist how you greeted them on your way in. Hiring managers could watch a candidate as they exit the interview premises. Conversely, some interviewees have some outrageous behavior such as starting to make calls or lighting up cigarettes right outside the premises. Remember to maintain official conduct until you are far from the premises.

Arrive about fifteen minutes early but do not show up at the interview door more than five minutes early

It goes without saying; you never want to be late for an interview. It is one of the biggest deal breakers if you cannot keep time on the first day. If you are not five minutes early, then you are late. It is recommended that you arrive early and get accustomed to the organization's ambiance. If you are uncontrollably running late, make sure to call and inform them of your delay. Always have the contact information of the person organizing your visit for such a reason, but make sure to overcome all obstacles to arrive at the scheduled time. It shows that you are punctual and you can be trusted with routines or to hit deadlines, or even to save time for the company. Conversely, arriving too early gives employers the first reason to start judging you from a negative light.

Close the interview the right way

Express your gratitude toward the interviewer for the interview as it comes to an end and restate your interest in the role. Feel free to make an inquiry on how long it would take before they could reach out. Finally, greet everyone in the room by the hand if possible and also use their name as this shows your attention to details and courtesy. Greeting other people in the outer office shows good manners as well, although it may not be a strategy per se. Remember to keep smiling until you leave the premises.

Send a thank you note after the interview

Thanking the hiring manager for the interview counts as an important part of your etiquette principles. It reminds the interviewers about you and shows them how courteous you are. Also, take this chance to clarify anything you feel you need to reiterate. Refer to anything that the interviewer said during the interview that intrigued you. Reiterate why you think you are fit for the position.

CHAPTER 6

INSIDE THE MIND OF AN INTERVIEWER

We'll let you in on a little secret. Interviewers don't want to have to interview. They'd rather you were already hired. Of course, especially in growing organizations, they'll have to interview people frequently, but in their ideal situation, these future interviews would always be for new openings. What interviewers really don't want is to have to interview candidates for the position that's currently open. Ever again.

It's not that they hate interviewing, although it's certainly not everyone's favorite task. And it's not simply that interviewing regularly for the same position can be a drain on an organization's resources. Interviewers also don't want to be proven wrong. They don't want to be the person who recommended hiring someone whose performance turns out to be lackluster. They don't want to be the person who recommended hiring someone who later needs to be fired. They don't even want to be the person who recommended someone who quits after ten months.

Succeeding in job interviews involves understanding both sides of the conversation, your own and that of the people who want to fill the open position. If you can manage to think like your interviewers, you will be able to speak directly to their concerns and put yourself that much closer to landing a great job.

In order to understand what's going on in the minds of hiring managers and your potential bosses, it can be helpful to think about how the process often goes wrong. Here are a few profiles of people we've worked with over the years. To be clear, none of these profiles represents a single real person, but they're characteristic of many coworkers whom we've known. Each also indicates an interview process that could and should have gone differently.

The square peg. The square peg might have been great in the interview setting, but he can't actually do the job. To the interviewer, his previous experience seemed highly relevant, but it turned out to be insufficient for the present job. His coworkers might appreciate his water cooler banter, but his bosses must double-check or reassign most of his work. What's worse, the extra coaching and training that they provide don't seem to help. In worst-case scenarios, his employers have to fire him in order to protect their workflow, and this brings down office morale. Suddenly, people who didn't work closely with this misaligned employee are thinking, *Why are people being fired randomly? Is* *my job at risk? Maybe I should start looking for a more secure position myself.*

The slacker. Unlike the square peg, the slacker may be perfectly capable, but she doesn't seem to do much of anything. She can't be bothered to learn the details of a project before an important meeting with a client. She sometimes closes the door to her office and chats with her mother all day. (Office doors don't block out noise *that* well.) When she's in a meeting, she "secretly" plays games on her iPhone. (It is wholly obvious when you're checking your work email and when you're on Facebook.) To make matters worse, the slacker's inaction upsets her coworkers, whose jobs are now harder than they were before she was hired. They're silently aware that the slacker is being paid a salary to do nothing at all.

The troublemaker. The troublemaker is often capable, and he usually does the work that is asked of him. But he does something else that is certainly not asked of him. He creates unnecessary tension in the workplace. This may be done in the form of subtle (sometimes less-than-subtle) gossip: "Do you think Mark is gunning for a promotion? I heard he had coffee with the VP of finance yesterday." Or "I'm pretty sure this new so-called security protocol is actually a system to keep track of how much time we spend at our desks." This person complains about his coworkers, office policies, and employee pay, but always to other employees and never to someone who actually has the authority to answer his questions or remedy the problem. This person is rarely fired for failing to complete his work, but he's also less likely to be given a second chance if he makes a mistake. For most employers this is an even bigger disaster than it seems. The toxic culture created by this person makes his coworkers dissatisfied; indeed, sometimes these employees leave, giving the troublemaker a chance to begin again with new hires.

The achiever. The achiever is more than capable, highly engaged, even respectful of her bosses and coworkers. She's a dream employee except for one major issue: she wants more recognition, a better title, and better pay and she wants these things faster than the organization can accommodate. The achiever may do wonderful things and do them quickly, but she jumps ship and signs with a competitor as soon as she has new accomplishments to display. Suddenly, the organization's top competitor has a great employee, while they themselves are back to hiring.

The prima donna. Watch out. The prima donna may be a good, even a talented, employee but his performance is out of line with his self-perception. Like the achiever, he wants a raise and a promotion, but unlike the achiever, he has an unrealistic sense of the demand for his skills. He may not want to leave his job (indeed, he may be unable to do so), but he demands as much as he can while he waits for something better. A prima donna doesn't necessarily produce further rounds of hiring, but if your interviewer is an experienced hiring manager, they will do their best to avoid hiring this character. A prima donna creates tension. His manager is always saying no or bending over backwards to give him what he wants, like the best office or best projects. And if he gets what he wants and is paid more than his equally effective peers, his coworkers may become aware of that inequality and feel less satisfied with their own situations. He's also often the first person out the door when the economy goes sour, because cutting his salary from payroll is the best bang for the buck.

The job hopper. The job hopper also shares an important trait with the achiever. She's a competent worker, but she's not fully committed. She questions, Am I meant to check tax returns or should I be in a forest in Canada, studying the migratory patterns of rare birds? Or perhaps her boyfriend has a job offer across the country, and she wants to follow. The job hopper leaves as soon as it's convenient for her, regardless of how her schedule fits with her employer's needs.

These are caricatures, of course. Good interviewers don't try to force people into boxes. And there can be good reasons to act in each of these ways. Some are truly great reasons, like trying to achieve your real earning potential or supporting a loved one as they take up a new career. The important thing to keep in mind is that interviewers don't want to have to hire more often than needed for the same position. It's their task to determine not simply whether you have the right experience, an excellent degree, or a winning personality; they need to know that you'll serve the organization's larger interests.

What Type of Employee Are You?

To determine what kind of employee you are, a good interviewer will try to glean several pieces of information. Some of these pieces of information are really important. We call these *major considerations*. Nearly all interviewers think about all of the major considerations, and they think about them for nearly all job candidates. The other pieces of information that an interviewer wants to learn are *minor considerations*. Only certain interviewers care about the minor things, they may care about them only for certain jobs, and they may not think about them for all candidates.

All of these considerations are reliant on one thing: that you come across as being accurate during the interview. Interviewers need assurance that you are self-aware and that you are accurately describing your experience. If they think you're talented at saying what you think they want to hear, or that your self-perception is wildly different from the way others perceive you, they won't believe anything you have to say. Show yourself to be a reliable source of information by sharing examples that back up your claims.

Major Considerations

From the standpoint of any organization, having to fire and then hire again is much worse than having to hire again because someone quit. Firing employees is unpleasant and costly, and it lowers morale. For this reason, the major considerations are competency, fit, and interest. If new employees don't meet the basic requirements for these considerations, they put their organizations at risk.

<u>Competency</u>

Basic competency is often the first quality that an interviewer tries to evaluate. It's good to remember that the evaluation of your competency begins before any representative of the organization shakes your hand or calls you on the phone. Before any interview, someone in the organization (usually multiple people) reviews your cover letter and resume. During this initial review, they ask themselves, "Can this applicant do the job?" And in order to answer this question, they'll look for relevant experience, knowledge, and the presence of particular skills.

If you're like many people (remember the obviously-strong-candidate approach?), you may be thinking that you spent hours and hours on your resume and it already explains your skills and abilities perfectly well, thank you very much. Why would an interviewer ask you about the same facts that you carefully listed for them already?

In a perfect universe, landing a job would be a simple matter of sending a resume. Alas, this is not the case. Resumes have a few key faults. What's more, the language of resumes is highly, if sometimes intentionally, ambiguous: the same description of last summer's internship often masks wildly different levels of experience or proficiency. And finally—and it's unlikely that this refers to you—small numbers of people out and out lie on their resumes.

Interviewers are aware of these faults. And for this reason, they will usually ask questions about how long, how often, and at what level you have actually performed the tasks and duties that you described on your resume. How long did it take you to become a spreadsheet expert? Was that successful branding campaign on social media entirely your effort or did you make important contributions as part of a team? You don't need to have learned everything already, but you do need to be able to speak clearly and effectively about what you know and how you hope to develop in the future.

The final thing to keep in mind about the ambiguity of your resume is that interviewers often test areas that seem like potential weaknesses. For instance, if the job posting mentions that effective employees will need to use Excel macros and you don't include anything about macros in your cover letter or resume, you will need to be prepared to answer a question about your ability or experience in this area. You needn't be an expert in macros, of course, to convey your general competence or your willingness to learn, but good preparation will lead you to expect this very question.

Fit

We've been throwing around the term "fit," but what does it actually mean? Fit is a catchall word to describe the fact that organizations want employees who can adapt easily to their roles, be successful, and contribute to the overall office culture. Fit is an elastic term. It means different things in different contexts.

Fit is sometimes a matter of the job in question. If a company is hiring a customer service representative, they may search for someone who is warm, supportive, and patient. These same qualities might ill serve someone who is a federal prosecutor. (No offense to federal prosecutors!) What's more, if an organization publicly espouses certain values, like its low environmental impact, a warm person who volunteers for local river clean-up days might be an even better fit.

Asking Questions

A survey by CareerBuilder in 2012 found that 32% of hiring managers reported that not asking good questions is one of the most detrimental mistakes job applicants make during an interview. Generally speaking, employers feel that if you don't have some prepared questions that are relevant to the job or company, then you might not really be interested in the job.

In my own experience in interviewing people for jobs, I would have to agree with the above survey. Time and time again I experienced people who did really well in the interview, but when it came time for them to ask questions, they either had no questions to ask, or the questions they asked were poor choices.

You might be thinking then, "What are the best questions I could ask at the end of an interview?" Similarly, "Which questions should I avoid?" In this chapter I will outline some possible responses to each of these questions.

Asking the right questions can help show the interviewer that you have prepared for the interview and that you are serious about this job. Employers respect people who want to know more about the job or the company. It should also be noted that asking questions provides another opportunity to sell you. In considering which questions you might ask, it is important for them to be positive, rather than asking a question that might be viewed in a negative manner by the employer. For example, it would make more sense to ask about the company's mission statement then it would to ask why their profits were down (if in fact you knew this kind of information).

The following provide some examples of questions that would be appropriate to ask in most job interviews:

What do you see as some changes that will be occurring in your organization over the next five years?

How would you describe the leadership style in your company?

What are the major skills and personal traits you are looking for in this job?

What are some immediate challenges you see as being addressed by the person fulfilling this job?

Why do you like working here?

Are there any aspects of this job that we haven't discussed here today that you think I should know about?

What sort of person is most successful in your company?

Does this company offer or support continued education or training?

What is the next step in the interviewing process? It would also be appropriate to ask for the timelines in this process if they are not given to you.

At some point, would it be possible to receive a tour of the company?

What is the most important thing you are looking for in hiring new employees?

The above questions provide examples of some questions you might ask at the end of an interview. I would suggest that you add any other questions that are important to you to this list.

After you do this, select 5 - 6 questions that are most important to you. Remember, this is also an opportunity for you to be assessing whether you really want to work for this company.

After you ask each question, don't hesitate to summarize what is said to you, or even ask further questions related to what you have been told. This demonstrates good listening skills which is an important aspect of success in almost any job. If there is strong conversation following any question, it might be advisable to cross a few questions off your list. Two or three questions with some follow-up discussion are better than a barrage of final questions with little or no discussion.

In considering the questions you might ask at the end of an interview, there are some that you should avoid. The following provides some sample questions that you should avoid during an interview (unless the answer is critical to you accepting the job, and even then you have to ask yourself whether it would be better to first be offered the job before asking the question).

Don't ask about salary, benefits, time off, etc. (these can all be discussed further once you have actually been offered the job.

Don't ask what the company does (this is information that you should have researched before the interview).

Similar to this, don't ask any questions that you could have simply Googled before the interview to find the answer.

Don't ask how quickly you can be promoted.

Don't ask whether the company does background checks.

Don't ask questions that relate to your personal needs as opposed to the needs of the company (for example, don't ask if you can have every Saturday off because you play golf).

Don't ask if the company monitors employees' emails.

Don't ask about any rumors or "dirt" you might have heard about the company.

Don't ask if you can do this job from home (unless of course, you expected that this was a part of the job description)?

Don't ask how many warnings does a person receive before getting fired?

As the interview ends, thank the interviewer (once again referring to him or her by name). This is another opportunity for a firm handshake and a smile. If you had some interaction with a receptionist or secretary before the interview, it would be appropriate to say something along the lines of "It was a pleasure meeting you." to this person before you leave the building if it is convenient.

CHAPTER 7

LINKEDIN

LinkedIn can be used as a job search tool, where you can apply for positions or contact potential employers directly, but LinkedIn is so much more than this and can be set up so that people contact you directly about opportunities; this is where the power really is.

Setting up LinkedIn correctly will give you much more online exposure, making you more visible to recruiters and potential employers.

LinkedIn Privacy and Settings

It's important you set up LinkedIn privacy and settings correctly. Follow these steps for maximum online exposure.

At the top right-hand side of your LinkedIn home page, hover over your profile picture icon and click 'Manage' next to 'Privacy & Settings'.

Privacy

After you click on 'Manage'. Click on 'Privacy' near the top of the screen.

Profile Privacy

- Click 'Edit your public profile' (The public profile options page will appear)

- Click 'Create your custom URL' and enter your name or as close to it as possible to create your unique URL.

- Click the button next to 'Make my public profile visible to everyone'

- Ensure all the boxes are ticked then click 'save' and back on your browser.

New or Existing Profile

If you are setting up your profile for the first time you'll see editable sections where you can add the relevant information to your profile. However if you are editing your profile you can do this directly from your existing profile page.

Important Note

LinkedIn is a business-networking tool and therefore you need to make sure your profile is visible to everyone. Sometime individuals will not upload a profile picture, or hide certain parts of their profile. This is a mistake if you are looking for work.

It is recommended that you switch on all visibility settings and ensure you complete every section when setting up your profile.

The following should be completed.

Personal information

- Insert your name in CAPITAL LETTERS

- Add a photo

- Add your job title followed by your company slogan or personal specialism such as "Professional Writer"

- Add your location

- Add your email address

- Add your phone number

- Add your location

- If you have a Twitter account, add it here

- Add your company website and LinkedIn profile URL

Additional Info

- Add Interests, be sure to add at least five.

- Add Personal Details.

- Add Advice for people to contact you.

Top tip: Ensure your interests are personal rather than work focused. People are also interested to know what you do outside of work.

Skills and Endorsements

Top tip: As well as adding professional skills ensure you include personal ones. People want to get to know you out of the working environment, so add skills that help to build greater rapport.

Courses

Top tip: In addition to courses, you can also add any training and coaching you have received. As before ensure these are both professional and personally focused.

Volunteer

Top tip: Add charitable organization that you are involved with

Languages, Publications & Projects

Ensure these 3 sections are completed as much as possible.

Groups

Top tip: Join groups you are interested in and groups you think your target audience is interested in. Many of your future connections will come from the groups you are a member of.

Influencers

Top tip: Follow influencers, news articles and companies that you are interested in and those you think your target audience will be interested in. Many of your future connections will come from people who follow the same influencers/topics as you.

CHAPTER 8

THE TEN MOST IMPORTANT INTERVIEW QUESTIONS AND HOW TO ANSWER THEM

1) Tell me something about yourself.

What the interviewer actually means is: *"What do you have to offer me?"*

Most interviewees believe that this is one of the most challenging questions an interviewer could ask. It is actually a great open-ended opportunity to share your best features. That said, resist the urge to praise yourself to the heavens. Keep it short and limit your answer to the features that you think will be most beneficial to the employer's business. For instance, you may have both technical computer skills and salesmanship skills. But if you're applying for a position which will require you to deal mostly with the technical aspect of computers, then stick to selling your computer skills.

Fight the inclination to present your whole autobiography. Instead, keep your answer short by providing a brief background and highlighting some of your most notable accomplishments.

Connect your educational background with the current position that you're holding. Make sure you cover your educational and career background and your most recent job experience. It is important that you express how your career has taken a logical advancement.

"I grew up in Connecticut and moved to New York where I studied Fine Arts and Art History at NYU. Straight out of college, I got a job at as an art curator at ____. Working in this job allowed me to learn a great deal about my chosen field and to cultivate my skills and knowledge as well as my stamina, my social skills, and my salesmanship skills. From there, I was able to obtain a senior position at _____. That's where I was truly able to develop my managerial skills as well as my ability to handle high-profile projects and manage budgets up to $1 million. Right now, I believe that all the skills and experiences that I've gathered throughout the years make me a suitable candidate for a position in your company. I intend to prove that today. Do tell me, what are the qualities you are seeking in an ideal applicant for this job position?"

With this answer, you were able to answer the interviewer's actual question: "What do you have to offer me?"

The things you are able to offer him are:

- your excellent stamina

- your social skills

- your salesmanship skills

- your managerial skills

- and your ability to manage million-dollar projects and budgets

2) Why do you want to work in this company?

Why indeed? While your true answer may be because you need something from the company (a salary, stability), make it seem as though it's the company that needs something from you.

For this question, mention the features of the company that appeal to you the most. Discuss how the company is the perfect place for you. In other words, show the interviewer why you will fit right in. Proceed to talk about the skills that you possess, which will enable you to benefit from the company while at the same time allowing the company to benefit from you. Demonstrate that you are eager for an opportunity to contribute.

"I'll go ahead and say right out that I'm thrilled with the idea of working in this company. I am seeking an opportunity where my skills will be put to good use and I think that this is the perfect place for me to apply and demonstrate my expertise. For instance, I am very interested in being a part of your company's current project: _____. I am positive that with my experience in cutting costs and maximizing revenues, I can contribute a great deal to this project's success."

3)   What makes you certain that you're qualified for this position?

When answering questions like this, you need only to remember that your contribution to a company is often only measured through two things:

- Money
- Time

Therefore, show your interviewer how you can help your employer increase the value of either or both. Thinking of yourself as a product, this is the time where you answer the interviewer with your benefits as opposed to your features.

"I believe that, considering my experience and skills in my previous job as a _____, I can aid you in saving time by ensuring that the workplace functions smoothly and productively. Coupled with my diligence and skills in negotiation, I also believe that I can lower *our* department's costs while increasing the revenues. By implementing _____, I was able to increase the revenue of (name of previous company you've worked for) by up to 25% in just 4 months' time. I see no reason why I shouldn't be able to do a similar thing for this company, *should I be provided with the opportunity* to work here."

4) Why did you leave your last job?

This can be translated to: If you were doing so well there, why did your employers allow you to leave? Is there anything about you that we should be wary of?

When answering questions similar to this, make it a point to present the facts as briefly as possible and to concentrate on the future. Don't dwell too long on the subject as this may cause your interviewer to grow suspicious. Emphasize that your departure from your previous company/employer was on good terms.

If the hiring manager was impressed with your CV and you were able to leave a great first impression, he'll be secretly hoping that you were not the problem. However, he'll want to have an idea as to how you conducted yourself during the departure. This means you'll have to provide some indication that you handled your departure professionally. How do you do this? By offering references.

Never say anything negative about your former company/employer/colleagues. Don't mention the involvement of other people in your departure. Moreover, refrain from giving more than one reason for leaving your previous job.

Take a look at this example:

"Actually, I've been seeking an opportunity to demonstrate and develop my skills. I'm not certain I would've been able to do this at my previous position. I left on good terms but right now, I'm here because I am certain that I possess the necessary skills to further my career at your institution."

This is a great answer and no one would even suspect that the speaker left a previous employer on bad terms. It's not as though he/she has told a blatant lie. The speaker merely chose to provide an ambiguous, yet smart, response which focuses on the future.

5) What was the most difficult situation that you've encountered and how did you handle it?

Read between the lines. What the interviewer actually wants to know is this: "If you were already working for me, will you crack under pressure and take the whole team down with you?"

Understand that your interviewer is trying to determine your critical thinking and problem-solving skills.

This is the kind of question which calls for one of your on-the-job "war stories." Although you may have encountered and sailed through a bunch of challenging situations, pick the one that is most closely related to the job position that you're applying for. Ask yourself: *What are the problems that I am most likely to encounter in this line of work?* Then determine how you can tie that up with your past experience.

In answering this type of question, concentrate on highlighting your transferrable skills rather than your technical skills. The best skills you can emphasize are your creativity, resourcefulness, and perseverance.

6)   What are your greatest strengths?/What are your greatest weaknesses?

When answering questions about your strengths, the trick is to fit them with the requirements of the position and the unspoken needs of your employer. Ask yourself: *Which of my traits will make my potential employer look good? Which of my skills will make his job easier for him?*

As for weaknesses, don't go so far as denying that you have any. Instead, mention your strengths first and mention lots of them. After that, state only one weakness. Choose the weakness which has the *least* to do with your target job position. For instance, you can admit that you're not very good with numbers if the job you're applying for doesn't really require you to deal with numbers on a regular basis. Don't elaborate on your weakness. Keep it brief and straight to the point. Never mention how this will potentially affect your work performance.

Another trick is to mention a weakness that is actually a "strength in disguise".

Example:

"Perhaps my greatest weakness is that I would sometimes grow impatient with coworkers concerning delays in their part of the task. It's just that missing deadlines bother me a lot."

After this, say no more as though indicating that you're prepared to move on to the next question.

7) What is your most notable accomplishment?

Whatever accomplishment that you choose to mention should be in line with the target position that you're applying for. You may have a long list of accomplishment and some of them may seem smaller than others. That said, don't measure your accomplishments according to *your* standards. Instead, measure them according to the company's needs.

Even so, if the greatest concern of the company you're applying for is how to gain public exposure, then mentioning the first accomplishment would benefit you more than mentioning the second one.

While talking about your accomplishment, convey genuine passion and pride through your voice and body language.

8) What are your future goals?

The reason why interviewers ask this question is because they want to know if you intend to stick around or if you're just trying the position on for size until something better comes along. A high employee turnover rate is costly for a company. This increases expenses associated with hiring and training. Regardless of the truth, your answer should focus on the target job position and the company's wellbeing.

Example:

"I intend to grow with a well-established company. I believe that a company like this will provide me with an opportunity for continuous career growth and will enable me to assume more responsibilities in the future as I continue to contribute to the organization's success."

9) How do you handle competition?

What your interviewer actually wants to know is that you have a positive attitude when it comes to competition. Employers are looking for employees who are up to besting the business competition. Thus, your answer should reveal that you embrace competition not only because you like winning but also because you recognize its positive effects on the business/organization.

Example:

"I would describe myself as a competitive worker. I believe that some competition can be healthy in the workplace as it brings out the best in everyone. Ultimately, competition can benefit the organization as a whole."

10) How much should we pay you?

This question is like the blade of a guillotine hanging over your head all throughout the interview. It's a question you're afraid to ask but would really, really want to know the answer to. It's a question that your interviewer will inevitably bring up although deep down, you wish he wouldn't. That's because both the interviewer and the applicant are aware that whoever brings up the figure first places himself at a vulnerable position for negotiating. Nevertheless, your interviewer might try to sneak the question in through an inquiry similar to this: *"How much are you making in your current job?"*

What do you tell him then?

Ask yourself these two questions:

- How much are you worth?
- What is your practical range?

Prior to showing up at the interview, make it a point to research your *market value*. That is, the going rate for a professional with your experience and skills. You can search for the figures online or look it up in professional journals related to your field.

The *practical range* refers to the minimum amount that you need to support your lifestyle.

To arrive at a range that you won't be sorry for, bracket the income range so that it slightly goes above the upper range of your market value. It must also be higher than your practical range.

Example:

If, according to your research, your market value is $76,000 -
$83,000, and based on your calculations, your practical range is
about $77,000, then tell the interviewer that your salary range is:
$79,000 – $86,000.

Important: In general, you must avoid the topic of salary until
you have been completely informed about the scope of the job
and until the interviewer has gained a complete understanding of
your qualifications. Delay salary talk until you reach the final
interview and until you're certain that you've convinced the
employer that his company needs you.

The Post-Interview Phase

So the interview is over. What should I do next?

Don't spend the post-interview phase waiting for the phone to
ring. Instead, use it for drafting a professional thank you letter to
your would-be employer. Apart from being a traditional act of
courtesy, a thank you letter will ensure that your application
becomes more prominent in your employer's mind. If you were
unable to close the sale with your closing statement during the

interview, this is the opportunity to do it.

A thank you letter is a business letter and not a note or a postcard. It should be printed or emailed. It should contain about four paragraphs.

Start off by thanking the interviewer and stating how pleased you were to meet him. Next, express your excitement over the possibility of working in his company. Include a summary of the highlights of the interview. Remind the interviewer of your selling points. Finally, in the closing statement, restate your understanding of when you expect to obtain a response from the employer.

If you were interviewed by more than one interviewer, make sure that each of them receives a different version of the letter.

View a sample of an effective thank you letter on the next page.

Laura Green

12345 Lakewood Ave.

Chicago, Illinois 60640

Telephone: 000-000-0000

Fax: 000-000-0000

Email: lauragreen@gmail.com

Mr. Paul Smith

Chief Nurse

Mercy Hospital and Medical Center

2525 S Michigan Avenue

Chicago, Illinois, 60616

Dear Mr. Smith,

Thank you for the opportunity to interview for the position of staff nurse. The vitality and intelligence of everyone I spoke with at your offices left a strong impression on me. I am extremely grateful for the warmth and sincerity by which my application was received. I am also thankful for the interest shown in me.

I am thrilled at the prospect of working at Mercy Hospital and Medical Center. You have established a solid team, which I would like so much to be a part of.

I was very pleased with our conversation and especially excited about the idea of the _____ project, which I believe will positively transform patient care. I learned a great deal from that experience and I wish to apply all that I've learned at Mercy Hospital and Medical Center.

Thank you very much again for the stimulating and productive interview. I look forward to hearing from you, as agreed upon, within the next two months.

Sincerely,

Laura green

CHAPTER 9

PREDICTING THE QUESTIONS

The worst part of any job search is the unknown involved with the process overall from top to bottom. Not knowing if you will be called at all, not knowing if you will get a job interview after the call, not knowing how the interview went or if you will get an offer after the job interview. Part of the unknown of the interview itself is what you will be asked and this unknown can be quite scary. However, much of this can be predicted with some digging on your own.

The digging that you must do is to get to know the job itself and get to know what would be the potential questions you might be asked. It would stand to reason that a janitorial job interview may have different questions than that of a cashier, right? Different strengths are necessary and different job pitfalls should be made clear, meaning different questions would be asked.

In order for you to know what might be asked you could start by asking yourself what may be necessary for someone to be able to complete this job successfully? To answer these question let's pretend you are applying for the role of a customer service agent at a large cable company. You could immediately say that the first necessary skill would be the ability to provide quality service, preferably over the phone.

This would be where you start to connect the past experiences and situations you have been in with the potential questions that may be asked. In addition to providing service over the phone another potential question could be about your experience in working in a production environment. This is to say an environment that moves at a quick pace and one that insists on you working fast with a purpose.

More questions could potentially be asked along these lines but this gives you a good start on seeing where these questions could go. Once you have decided on a few different avenues those questions could take you can move on to the next potential question. This set of questions has to do with your perception of what a successful candidate for the position would look like?

In this scenario you should try to picture what a good candidate would look like by picturing what a successful employee would look like. Do you think it would take patience to be able to deal with all of the customer demands levied on the customer service department at a cable company? Wouldn't a successful candidate need to be able to communicate clearly on a personal and professional level with customers?

If these are the qualities that would stand out for a successful candidate then you need to find examples from your past that show your ability to do these things. While you are on this step it is also a good idea to consider what the unsuccessful habits or qualities of a candidate would be. What would be something that would doom someone to fail at this job?

Take a personal story on this from my past as a corporate trainer at a major corporation starting the first day of a new class of new employees. We were going around the room introducing ourselves and telling the group what our ideal job would be. This one particular new employee stated his name and then said that his degree was in a laboratory science and that his dream job was to work in a lab all by himself.

There was no problem in particular with this dream as it was a good explanation from someone who had a dream to pursue. The issue was that the job was one where the individual would be working all day on the phone taking calls from angry customers in relation to insurance claims. Immediately I knew that this fit was not going to work and the individual quit within weeks of working claims. He was a very bright and engaging young man, but the job was a terrible fit for what he wanted to do.

This bleeds over into the next potential question you should ask yourself, why would people leave this position? In the instance my previous job mentioned above it would be a variation of what happened with that individual. People came to our company who had degrees but did not have any profession in mind, many weren't happy on the phones all day and they left.

What will happen during the hiring and training process is that you will be repeatedly sold on the amazing nature of the company and how it can help you. People will tell you how incredible the company treats people and much of it may be true, but the fact of the matter is really quite simple. Aside from a company that is growing too fast, you are being hired because someone else didn't work out or didn't want the job anymore.

In the case of the customer service department at the cable company you may be facing many of the same pitfalls as the company I previously worked for. Lack of patience, lack of communication skills and an environment that was too fast paced were all complaints that were regularly fielded. Consider these and be sure to emphasize how you would or could overcome these potential problems.

This then transitions nicely into the final question you should ask yourself about the job, which is what is the most difficult part of the job? Would it be answering the phones all day or dealing with angry customers one after the other? There could be any number of potential trouble spots and you need to try to dig in on what the hardest could be.

The beauty of this for today's day in age is that you have access to the internet and can do a simple search for the company and people who have left. The complaints aren't always 100% accurate, but if you keep seeing the same complaints over and over it is probably a difficulty that should be considered. Being prepared to explain how you could overcome this could put you over the top of all of the applicants.

Remember that you have the control over your answers and can phrase them in such a way to show your ability to do the job. Predicting the questions can give you a jumping off point to consider what might be asked so that you can consider what situations you should be prepared to explain from your past. With interviews preparation can put you over the top when you do it smartly and correctly.

12 Most Common Job Interview Questions and How Best to Answer Them

No two job interviews are the same. But job interviews generally follow a similar pattern with similar questions. So, you need to arm yourself with the kind of questions you should expect and the best response for each question. Recruiters are also aware of the fact that there are many blogs out there with the title 'How to Answer Job Interview Questions' and they can tell when you are merely reciting what you have memorized from another source. In other words, this is a guide on how to answer the questions and not exactly how you should answer the questions. I am giving you a pattern and some strategies; for you to tailor these down to fit your own personal experiences.

Here are some of the most common job interview questions and how to answer them:

Tell us about Yourself:

This is usually the first question and asked by practically all job interviewers. You should expect it and prepare for it beforehand. It is however, not an invitation for you to summarize your resume; they have seen your resume already and still want to know more about you. You should talk about your background; and by background, I do not mean your family background and personal life history. Don't mention your marital status or any other personal matters, including religious and political views. No matter how beautiful your family story may be, do not share it because that is not what they are wanting to hear. Summarize your educational history in not more than three sentences, talk about your professional experience if you have any. This is the time to clarify the gaps on your resume if you have any. Talk about your skills as they relate to the position and say a thing or two about your personality. All these should be in line with the role you are being interviewed for. And you should stop talking if you are cut short while you are still answering it.

What Do You Consider to Be Your Biggest Professional Achievement?

This question can be a tough one especially if you just graduated from college and haven't had any professional experience. Preparing for this question will go a long way to affect how you will respond to it. This is an opportunity for you to talk about your internship experience if you have any and what you consider to be your biggest achievement in the process. Do not just give a vague mention of the achievement, give a vivid description of what you actually did and how it helped the company or team you worked with. Talk about results; that's what the recruiter wants to hear.

What are your Biggest Weaknesses?

For every question you will answer, remember that you should provide answers in line with what you are interviewing for. If you are asked what your biggest weaknesses are, make sure that whatever you state your professional weaknesses, not your general weaknesses as a person. Another thing to note is that at each stage of the interview, you are marketing yourself and you shouldn't say anything that will vilify you. You should not tell lies. However, if your biggest professional weaknesses are not something you wish to disclose, you should consider saying something else whether it is the biggest of your weaknesses or not. Pick a weakness of yours and embellish it in such a way that it will eventually turn out interesting. Consider this example from www.inc.com :

Interviewer: What are your biggest weaknesses? Interviewee: My biggest weakness is getting so absorbed in my work that I lose track of time. Every day I look up and realize everyone has gone home! I know I should be more aware of the clock, but when I love what I am doing, I just can't think of anything else.

In other words, your biggest weakness is that you will put in more hours at work and that will be considered as strength for the company.

You can also talk about a weakness you are currently working on and give brief details about the steps you have taken to improve in that area. That way, the interviewer will consider you as someone who goes out of their way to look for solutions to problems.

What are your Biggest Strengths?

This is practically the opposite of 'What are your biggest weaknesses' and you have to be careful with answers as well. You should state what your biggest strengths are but do it in such a way that you will not present yourself as a superhuman. Simply say what your actual professional strengths are and demonstrate with a short description how that strength has helped solve a work-related problem in the past. For instance, if your biggest strength is effective communication, give an instance of when you used that skill to get something done or get other people to do things. And remember to give a sincere answer.

What Motivates you?

There is no right or wrong answer to this question. But then this is a job interview and you need to impress your interviewer. So, like every other question you will answer on this interview, tailor your answer to the role you are interviewing for. You should mention positive things like having to meet deadlines, being a part of a team, being a leader, discovering and learning new things etc.

Where Do You See Yourself in the Next Five Years?

This question can be somehow challenging, especially if you do not have long term career plans. But always remember that you are answering in relation to the position you are interviewing for and avoid mentioning anything outside this. This is not the time to talk about the vacation you have been imagining or how much money you expect to have in your bank account by that time. Talk about how you intend to grow from the experience you will receive from the role and some value you expect to be adding to the company. Give realistic goals and how the position will enhance your chances of reaching them.

What do you know About this Company?

This is a straight forward question, which means that it is expected that you must have done your homework about the company. Describe what you have found out about the company in relation to their competitors and the industry at large. But do not mention if their competitors are doing better than them. Highlight how the company is doing, especially in the area of the position you are interviewing for and how you think it is the best place for you to pursue a career.

How Did You Find Out About this Opening?

This kind of question is another opportunity for you to show that you are interested in the company and not just interested in getting a job. Your response should be specifically about how you found out about the opening. Even if you learned about it through a random job search, try to tell them what caught your attention about this particular opening and how excited you were when received got an invitation for the interview.

What Type of Work Environment do you Prefer?

This shouldn't be a difficult one if you have done your homework about the company. Simply bring in the work culture of the company and how it connects to the position you are interviewing for. It shouldn't be about you alone but about how the kind of work environment you prefer will help you be more successful in your role and add value to the company.

Why do you Want this Job?

Well, why do you want the job? A very simple question, but the way you respond will go a long way to determine the outcome of your interview. Just like every other question you will answer, this should be about the role as well and your overall career growth and development. You should never say that you want the job because you are broke and need the salary. Whether this is the true situation or not, please never say it. Explain how the role and how it is represented in the company fits into your personal career plans. Explain how you think that the company has the kind of environment that will enhance growth and push you forward in your career.

What is your Salary Expectation?

This question can make you very uncomfortable and you may find yourself in between trying not to oversell yourself and also trying not to undersell yourself. If you mention a large salary, you could come across to the interviewer as arrogant. If you ask for a small salary instead, you could come across as undervalued and the quality of what you have to offer will be in doubt.

The best way to go about this is to know beforehand the average salary requirement of the position you are interviewing for. Do your research and find out what the position is worth. Then go ahead and give a salary range. Do not mention a specific amount; that would be too direct. Also let your interviewer know that you are flexible on the salary expectation and it is left for you to accept or reject what they will offer you. Another way to answer the salary expectation question is to tell the interviewer that you will be okay with the company's budget for the position. But if you say this, also make sure that you are willing to accept what they have to offer.

Why Should We Hire you?

This question sums up everything about the interview. "Now that you have told us all these, what other reason do you think that, out of all the candidates being interviewed for this position, we should hire you?" This is an opportunity for you to sell yourself. Emphasize not only how you can do the job, but how you can do it better than any other candidate. Talk about your most important skills and how you can produce results within the company culture.

CHAPTER 10

MAKE YOUR STORIES COME TO LIFE

I love doing improv with job seekers. It is so much fun, and although we aren't intending to be funny, we always end up laughing–at ourselves, at what was just said, at the situation. It is certainly a stretching experience to do improv. In the context of a coaching session, it feels very safe. It is just the two of us. If, at the end of this book, you want to venture out a little more, I recommend that you join an improv class to experience it in a group setting. Not all improv makes sense for the job search process. I've culled the list of games to ones that are very relevant to our world–increasing charisma by playing big, being intentional with your eye contact, and staying connected through mime. Jump on a video call with your coach. Or ask a friend to play some of these improv games with you. Through this process we learn a little more about ourselves as it forces to be right here, right now, present. Let's play!

Improve Games That Help with Body Control

Game: Play Big and Play Small

Imagine there are two chairs up on stage. You are sitting in one of the chairs and an improv partner is sitting next to you. The two of you are facing an audience. The lights are glaring in your eyes and you can see shadows of people sitting in the audience watching the two of you. Your job is to play big without saying a word or making a sound. Sitting on the chair with the use of communicating big with your body, you are to claim that space. Your improv partner next to you is playing small. Using his body, without saying a word, he is playing small. The goal is for you to play big and slowly transform to small over a period of 30 seconds. The teacher in the audience will tell you when it is 15 seconds and when it is time at 30 seconds. Your improv partner's goal is to do exactly the opposite. He is to play small and transform to big over 30 seconds.

Terri and I use video meetings for this game. She starts with being big and I start with being small. In 30 seconds, we switch back and forth from being big to being small.

You can do this at home. Place a chair in front of a mirror and play big. Put on a timer that signals at 30 seconds. And over that period, without saying a word, transform to play small. Pay attention to how you feel when you are playing big and when you are playing small. Try it!

When I asked Terri to explain what she did when she played big, this is what she said:

- I am sitting up

- My shoulders are back

- My legs are spread and out in front of me

- My arms are draped over the arms of my improv partner's chair

- I am looking directly ahead

- I am looking around directly into my partner's eyes

When I asked Terri to explain how she felt when she was playing big, this is what she said:

- Confident
- Big
- Aggressive
- In control
- In charge
- The boss

I asked Terri, what did you feel when you were playing small?

- Timid
- Scared
- Submissive
- Anxious
- Cautious

Give it a try. For an entire week, play big. And take note at how you feel.

Game: Control Your Eye Contact

Because we do not go through life looking in a mirror, we often aren't aware of how we communicate with our eyes. We may not know that our eyes might be moving constantly or that we might come across as staring. This improv game is one that helps us become aware of our eyes and gain control over what we want to communicate with them.

Imagine you are in a room with your hypothetical improv team. Half of the team, Team A, has a goal to give what they would consider to be intense or too-long eye contact. The other half, Team B, has a goal to avoid eye contact or give too-short eye contact. When the game starts, everyone is to walk around the room acting out their goal. You'll hear nervous laughter and all-out bursts of laughter as two Team A members have a staring contest. Then about 2 minutes into the game, the instructor tells everyone to switch. Team A's job is to avoid all eye contact and Team B's goal is to give intense eye contact. At around two minutes more, the teacher calls time.

In a coaching session, the coach's goal is to give intense eye contact and the client's goal is to give not enough, or fleeting eye contact. Then we switch after 30 seconds.

At home, you could ask a friend to play the role of the coach. Sitting across a table, designate someone to give intense and the other fleeting eye contact. Use a timer and switch after 30 seconds.

Then we debrief and ask to share what happened and what made them laugh, how they felt, which was the most comfortable for them. Typically, the answers are something like the below:

- If I am avoiding eye contact, it is uncomfortable when someone gives me intense eye contact. It feels like an invasion of my space. It feels too intense.

- But when I am the one giving intense eye contact, it is frustrating when someone is avoiding my eye contact.

- It is a bit more comfortable if I meet with someone

who is also giving intense eye contact, but if it goes too long, it feels uncomfortable.

- When I am avoiding eye contact and come across someone who is also avoiding, it feels good not to be stared at; however, I do not even see who that person was.

In a coaching session, I will share if I feel that the individual gives a comfortable amount of eye contact. It is a challenge over video conference, and the fact that we aren't looking in a camera at eye level and instead at the person on the screen. However, it is excellent practice since many job interviews are conducted over video conference.

This game helps people understand how it feels when appropriate intensity of eye contact is given. It gives people the opportunity to play around with too much and too little to have greater control over when it is just enough.

Game: Staying Connected Through Mime

A mime is an actor who is generally in black and white clothing, with white clown paint on their face. They act out different things without using their voice. Imagine you are standing in a large circle with other people and you are all mimes. One person starts by holding an imaginary object and doing something obvious with the object. It could be bouncing a basketball or kicking a soccer ball. He then passes or hands the object to his neighbor who then continues doing what his neighbor did with the object. Then he changes it up. Perhaps the basketball shrinks and become a tennis ball. That person then passes or hands the object to the next person. And it goes down the line.

As you can image, sometimes you have no idea what your partner just did. The actions aren't always obvious and you need to make sense of the action. And you'll also realize that it is fruitless to think of something to do ahead of time because you won't know what the object is until it is handed to you.

This game forces us to use our bodies in intentional ways to describe the object and do something with it. It also helps you learn how to not anticipate what you will do with the object because you have no idea in what form the object will come to you. Learning not to anticipate and just be in the moment is one of the most useful things improv can help with in the job search process. It drives out the habit of spinning in your own head. You must just be in the moment.

In a coaching session, I start with an object, do something obvious, and then hand it to the job seeker. She takes it, continues with what I was doing and then does something different and hands it back to me.

At home, you can ask a friend to do the same where you start with an object, do something obvious, and then hand it to your friend. She takes it, continues with what you were doing and then does something different and hands it back to you.

Here are a few ideas of things that you could do with your improv group, whether in a large group or in a pair:

- Eat a lollipop

- Eat a popsicle

- Eat an ice cream cone

- Throw a volleyball

- Throw a baseball

- Use a home phone

- Use a mobile phone

Improv Games That Help with Voice Control

Now that you have learned improv games that help you have greater awareness and control of your body, let's focus on your voice. When you combine body and voice control, you are on your way to making a very powerful in-person impression. Voice control is critical to get invited to a face-to-face interview. Many companies will first want to speak with you over the telephone before they make the investment in coordinating an in-person interview. And I've found that many job seekers aren't sure how they come across over the telephone. They think they are showing up in one way, but my impression of them is slightly, or sometimes very, different.

Many of my clients are across the nation so it is impractical to meet them in person. The first time I see them is always a wonderful surprise, as I'm seeing someone that I've grown to love over a period. It is always a wonderful surprise to finally see someone's animated face and not just an image, like a photo from their LinkedIn profile. And I am always surprised that the person is nothing like I had expected. Which goes to show that when we only speak with a recruiter, they also form an impression of what you look like that is often very different from what you actually look like. The idea is to control that impression as much as you can. Below are a few improv games you can play to gain greater voice control.

Because improv feeds off at least one other person, most improv games are best done within a pair or a group. Improv is an interactive sport. Here are a few improv games that you can play solo if you have a device that can record what you are saying (e.g., smartphone).

Game: Talking Fast and Slow

In high school, I was running for a state position for a national business organization. While I was practicing my speech, my dad kept saying, "Slow down!" It was a struggle to really slow it down. I thought it was so people could follow along with what I was saying; however, what I discovered is that we make assumptions about someone's competence by the speed of their speech. Research says that people who speak slowly appear to be more competent and intelligent.

Use your mobile device or another recording device for this game. Grab some nearby text and record yourself reading it. At first, read it fast, much faster than your normal speech rate, and record yourself. Then read the same page again at a rate slower than your normal speech rate. Play back both recordings and see the difference in how you come across speaking quickly and slowly.

In improv, comedians use voice control to support a certain character they are playing. They will speed up when it serves them. In the same way, you want to be mindful of the rate of your speech so that you support how you wish to come across. For the most part, you will be speaking slowly and clearly to support the fact that you are competent and in control.

Related to speed is the power of the pause. Pauses can be used wisely to make a point. Consider this sentence and placement of the pause: "That project was the turning point for our division. [pause] We saw revenues climb at a steady pace from that point. And I cannot emphasize how vital our cohesion was to our success. Without it [pause] we would have failed."

Try it on for size. For an entire day, be very deliberate in speaking slower than your normal rate and see how it feels. And throw in a few pauses [pause] to make a point.

Game: High and Low

Besides the speed of your speaking, the pitch is also important. Individuals who have a high vocal pitch are seen in a different way than individuals with a lower pitch. People who speak at a higher pitch come across as less confident. Conversely, people with a lower pitch come across as more confident, dominant.

Let's play another improv game with your recording device. Read another page from a book in a pitch that is slightly higher than your normal pitch and record yourself. Do the same and read with a slightly lower pitch than normal. Listen to both recordings and take note of how you come across.

Give it a go. Spend an entire day speaking in a lower pitch than your normal. How did that feel?

Another thing to think about is if you end your sentences on an up note–when your voice goes higher as if you are asking a question. I find that often people aren't aware when they tend to end their sentences on an up note. As with the speed and the pitch, the tendency may leave an impression that you don't want. Research shows that individuals who end their sentences on an up note come across as less confident and more subservient, always seeking approval. Of course, this is not necessarily the case if this is your tendency. Many of my clients who have this tendency are strong, assertive, and confident. They just aren't aware how they come across.

Controlling your voice in and of itself is helpful in the job search process as many of the screening interviews are done over the telephone–no visual used. Combined with body control, you now offer a very powerful package. Let us now mix it in with the stories that were created in the previously and put it all together.

Integrate Body and Voice Control with Your Character:

You

During Steve Martin's Masterclass, he encourages comedians to leverage what makes us unique, saying, "There is room for you." In his world, to use our uniqueness contributes to being hilarious. And that holds true for our work as well. To use our uniqueness to be amazing.

Sitting in a room with Jenny, an impressive Communications Specialist, I was heartbroken, as it was obvious to her (and everyone else) that the Vice-President was about to push her out. To me, she was amazing. And it was clear that this organization was not a great fit for her–her unique and creative, out-of-the-box ideas landed too often on glazed faces. Jenny soon left the company and took a job in a firm with the perfect culture for her. She is now the Director of Communications for a global financial services firm reporting to the CEO and creating the most innovative stuff in the field of corporate communications.

There is room for you. Let us mix in You by using improv. First by putting on the skin of someone who is completely out of character for you.

Game: Get Into Character

Let's have some fun and pull these things together with a few improv games. Let us try on a few skins of other people that may be very different from us. Take one of the characters below and imagine yourself putting on their skin. Say the below paragraph in that character using body and voice control to become the character. Try not to break and burst out in laughter. Stay in character. Practice what we've learned in body and voice control to become the person.

Say this paragraph in character. Watch YouTube clips of others in this persona to practice a few times and try it.

It is a beautiful day. The sun is shining and the birds are singing. I'm excited to be alive!

- 16-year-old Valley Girl from California–It's like so beautiful. Like totally kicking. Like the sun is amaaaazing. I'm so, like, you know, OMG, alive.

- Gun slinging, swaggering cowboy in the wild, wild west– (burst through the saloon doors, take a swig from your cigarette and flick it to the floor) Well, if it ain't a pretty day. Sun was shining in my eyes as I shot a bird singing. A good day to be alive.

- A cranky, crusty, pessimistic old man–Pffft. Don't give me all this crap about it being a beautiful day.

Stupid sun shining in my eyes. Damned birds singing. Shut up. Not a good day to be alive.

- A 30-foot giant–Fi fi fo fum. It's a beauuutiful day for some delicious bird. Cook it in the sun. Feed my big hungry belly to say alive.

- Martin Luther King, Jr.–I have a dream. One day, one beautiful day. The sun will shine and the birds will sing. We. Will. All. Be. Alive.

- A pirate–Avast you scurvy scum. Shiver me timbers, the sun's out. It's a blimey sunny day. Me burd danced the hampen jig. Son of a biscuit eater.

What Is Your Character? Create an Archetype

Now that we are donning the skins of other characters, let us talk about our own archetype for the interview: You. What is the skin that we will put on as we enter the interview space? The skin of You?

A few years back, I attended a coach training class. On the second day we did a remarkable thing. Carey Baker, instructor extraordinaire, pulled me on stage and asked everyone to throw out a few words or phrases of things people wanted to see more of from me. What was remarkable was that up until this point, we haven't spent a tremendous amount of time together. How could they possibly know me that well? Yet my fellow classmates were throwing out words and phrases at such a fast speed that someone had to write them down for me. This is the list:

- Adventure

- Break the rules

- Be brave

- Step out

- Say F*** YOU

Then Carey asked the group to think of a personality or an archetype that they would like to see me put on. Many archetypes were thrown out, but the one that really stuck with them (I had no say in the selection, by the way) was Motorcycle Mama.

Yes! That is perfect! Motorcycle Mama. We want more of Motorcycle Mama from you, Cara. Kick some ass. Jump on your hog and screech out of here, leaving a trail of dust in our faces.

I've since renamed this archetype to be Badass Motorcycle Mama, and over the years have put on this skin when I've needed to be big and a bit of a badass. And over time, this persona has become more a part of me. So, what is your archetype?

Here are a few archetypes of some of my clients.

- Oprah Winfrey

- Adonis the god of war

- Purring sexy black panther

- Pele, the fire goddess of the Hawaiian Islands

- James Bond

- Dr. Love

If you need help finding your archetype, send me a note, and let's get on the phone. I love helping people find their archetype, and you'll be amazed at how you can do this after a very short conversation.

It's Show Time – Let's Put It All Together

Put on your skin of You, your archetype. Answer the question,

"Tell me about yourself." Use your body control and your voice control. Get into the character, stand in front of a mirror, and now rehearse. How is it different in character? Bigger? Bolder? Many job seekers say that they are much more aware of how they come across. And even more important, they can control how they come across. Their stories are more vivid with pauses for effect. Using silence. To make a point.

Ask your coach or a friend to conduct a mock interview. Record the session. Go back and view it. Refine your pitch, your skit, your stories. Ensure that you are coming across as you intend. Powerfully you. You have the tools to show up in a very powerful way. A way that is authentic and true to you. Showing them that you are secure in who you are, what you stand for, and what you can accomplish for them. And with a new awareness of You, your archetype, the skin of which you don as you prepare for and enter conversations with a recruiter. What we've talked about up until this point is how you show up. But as we know, it takes two to tango. There is someone else in the conversation: the recruiter, or the hiring manager, or other members of the team that you will interact with along the way.

CHAPTER 11

COMMON PITFALLS

Failure stories. The interviewer will almost certainly ask you to describe a time when you failed in your career or life. Many people make the mistake of trying to spin the example as something that turned out very positive in the end. This is likely because it can hurt to talk about our failures and we want to make a good impression. However, interviewers actually *want* to hear your failure stories. They are expecting something substantial and impactful that. It should be something that was etched in your memory and *hurt*.

For example, when asked about your failure story, a poor story would be "the time you didn't efficiently use the marketing budget and wasted money." This would **not** be a good example because the marketing budget is already set. This failure did not cause much damage.

A better story would be the time you hired someone and realized they were a terrible fit for your culture, and subsequently fired them after five months. In the process, you wasted thousands of dollars, sucked time from managers, and hurt company morale. That is a painful and tangible example. You can, of course, still talk about what you learned from the experience, interviewers want to see that you learned through the failure.

A good, juicy failure story needs to have a real negative impact on others. If you did something wrong in your previous position but faced no consequences, then it is probably not sufficient. When you lose a client and your team suffers — that is bad. When you fail to meet a deadline and a project is canceled, that reflects poorly on you *and* the company.

In the end, this ties back to the leadership principle of taking *ownership*. Make sure to prepare two examples of failures and do not be afraid to speak transparently about your mistakes.

Dive Deep. The reason interviewers dig so deep into the details of your past is to make sure that you actually did what you said you did. The logic is that the best way to discover your true role and responsibility in a job is to grill you on the details. If you said that you were a "sales leader," they want to know the story of how you closed the biggest sales deal. Was your boss in the meeting with you? Did someone else do the contract negotiation? Or were you involved in every step of the negotiation on your own? The depth and scope of your responsibility will come to light through this storytelling.

People who prepare the least for interviews tend to break down when "dive deep" is tested. They get flustered because they are asked to justify their thinking and decision-making process. Frequently, interviewers will ask you, "Why did you decide to take that action? How did you analyze your options? Why did you not push back to your supervisor to try a different option?" You need to be able to explain the logic behind all of your examples.

Diving deep can also be required in the form of *tangible outcomes*. When you describe the size of your marketing budget, they want a number. When you talk about the ROI they also want to know that number. You can talk about your great sales achievement and share a number, but how does that compare to others in the company? How does your sales number compare to the target this year and also last year? Providing context and specific details to describe the impact you made is key.

When you prepare 30 different examples from your previous work, it is unlikely that you are going to remember all of the details and reasons for your decision making. Thus the best way to prepare is to limit the number of examples you prepare to five or six key stories in your career. This way, you will be able to dive deep every time.

Not Answering a Question. One of the biggest mistakes I see people make is when they cop out of answering questions. When you say "I don't know" or "next question please," then you will likely be disqualified immediately. I realize this sounds unfair at first and you might be thinking, *"How am I expected to know all of the answers?"*

This does not mean you have to have a perfect answer to every question. That is an impossible expectation, and interviewers realize everyone might answer differently. Rather, they are more interested in your thinking *process.* They want to know how you break down a problem and how you go about solving it, even if the answer is incorrect. Furthermore, interviewers expects interviewees to think on their feet.

If you need time to think about an answer, then you can simply ask the interviewer to give you one minute to think about it. There is nothing wrong with some silence as you contemplate. Also, you can always request to come back to the question later. Write it down so you do not forget. Whatever you do, the point is to make sure that you always provide some sort of answer!

Long Winded Answers. You will always have more to say than you actually need to. Let that one sink in for a second.

It's important that your answers are never more than a couple of minutes long. If they are, you will be seen as verbose, and it will be marked heavily against you. The challenge is that the interviewer is not going to give you any indication if they want you to stop talking. They will patiently sit there and listen to you while you dig your own grave.

This may sound a little bit harsh, but it's one of the most common traps. People tend to get nervous and ramble, which happens to all of us. To stop yourself from doing this, always use the STAR approach. Second, use a mental timer to keep your answer short and concise. If the interviewer wants more details, they will ask for more. Rather than assume what the interviewer wants to hear, give the concise version of what you're trying to say, and let them probe deeper if they are interested.

CONCLUSION

Thanks for getting this book. It's my firm belief that it will provide you with all the answers to your questions. Starting a new job can be exciting and nerve wracking. Meeting new people, going to new places, and starting out with a blank slate, are all things which can make you feel insecure and uncertain. Remember that the choice to begin a new position is a choice which was made to help you take steps forward in your career. The fact that you have gained a new position over hundreds of other applicants is a testament not only to your interview skills but you as a person. You were the best fit for the position!

Take time out to enjoy the transition phase of starting a new job or career. Pat yourself on the back and be grateful at the opportunity before you. There are many people who wanted the job you have and were not offered a position. Now is the time to focus on showing your company they made the right choice in choosing you as their star candidate.

Do not be surprised if the position you take shifts and changes over time. It can very well be that as the company gets to know your skills better, they may shift your duties slightly to give you the best chance at success. Be sure to communicate openly with your supervisors, while you continue your work efforts, to be certain you are remaining on the same thought path for your career and involvement in the company.

If you find yourself becoming interested in other aspects of the company do not be afraid to vocalize this fact. The more in tune you are with your goals and desires, and the more you communicate with your superiors, the easier it will be to transition into other positions if the opportunity arises. There is nothing wrong with realizing you desire a completely different career path down the line than what you have accepted. It is best to try and remain in a position, unless given a promotion or are moved by the company itself, for at least three years.

The reason for this is because every company likes to see longevity and commitment to the positions you have already taken. People who move from one position to another quickly are also more likely to jump ship. You do not want your new employer to lose faith in your loyalty and excitement for the position you have taken.

Continue to practice your interview skills even if you are happy within your current position. Take time to practice with friends, even acting as the interviewer, and keep your resume up to date. When you have been in a position for a while it can become way to easy to become complacent and lose touch with what an interview is like. Should you desire to apply for a position higher up within the company you may attempt to rely solely on your work merits. Doing this may keep you from being the shining star you were when you gained the position which started you in the company to begin with. Even though you have started the position of your dreams it is always helpful to remain on your game.

Even if you are happy to remain in your position for the rest of your life be sure to take time for yourself and stay excited about your job and the company. Take your vacation time when you can and allow yourself rest and relaxation. Working too much is an easy trap to fall into as people with flourishing careers often feel they are unable to take time off as they are too pivotal to the company function.

If you are constantly working and never taking time for your private life you will easily burn out and begin to hate the job you originally loved. Keeping the passion alive may require effort but it will not require as much effort as trying to rekindle the relationship you once had should it start to fizzle. Set clear boundaries with your work place when you take your position so you are clear about the expectations of the hours you are required to work. If possible, take time to reaffirm these boundaries if they are being crossed over time because it will be a necessary practice to keep your heart in your work.

Remind yourself over time what aspects of your job you love. Keep positive affirmations at the ready to continue providing a positive attitude for yourself. There will be bad days at your job as every job has difficulties. No place of employment is perfect but you can be extremely happy if you have taken the time to apply for positions which truly fit who you are.

Your job does not define who you are but it is a big aspect of the building blocks that make you. Being in a position which you find fulfilling and rewarding will help you in your career path forward and keep you in a positive and happy mindset in the workplace. That positivity will then transfer over to your colleagues and will create an all-around better atmosphere.

Be grateful for the new opportunity and rejoice in the fact that you have taken another step closer to your achieved dreams and goals. Your hard work has finally paid off and will continue to do so as you keep bringing all of the wonderful talents you pose to the table. Congratulations on your new position and look forward to the future you will manifest for yourself.

Remember, you should play up your strengths so that you will be viewed in a favorable way. That will help you greatly in the application process and make you a candidate who stands out.

All the best!!

www.ingramcontent.com/pod-product-compliance
Lightning Source LLC
Chambersburg PA
CBHW070347220526
45467CB00001B/275

9781707766116